12-18-6

THE OXHERDER

THE
OXHERDER
A ZEN PARABLE ILLUSTRATED

STEPHANIE WADA

With translations by Gen P. Sakamoto

GEORGE BRAZILLER / NEW YORK

Acknowledgments

I thank Mary Griggs Burke and the Mary and Jackson Burke Foundation for making the Burke Foundation handscroll of the *Ten Oxherding Songs* available for publication. I am also indebted to George Braziller and to Miyeko Murase, Special Consultant for Japanese Art at The Metropolitan Museum of Art, New York, who together came up with the idea for this book. Gen P. Sakamoto, adjunct professor of art history at Kean University, New Jersey, provided the excellent translations of the handscroll's poems, preface, and postscript. I am grateful to both Professor Sakamoto and Gratia Williams Nakahashi, Curator of the Mary and Jackson Burke Foundation, for reading and commenting on my manuscript and owe many thanks to Mary Taveras at George Braziller, Inc., for her organization and coordination of this entire project.

The *Ten Oxherding Songs* are reproduced from a handscroll dating to 1278,
during the Kamakura period (1185–1333), and executed in ink and color on paper.
Collection of the Mary and Jackson Burke Foundation.

Introduction © 2002 by Stephanie Wada

English translations of the *Ten Oxherding Songs* © 2002 by Gen P. Sakamoto

For information, please address the publisher:
George Braziller, Inc.
171 Madison Avenue
New York, NY 10016

Library of Congress Cataloging-in-Publication Data:
Wada, Stephanie.
The oxherder : a Zen parable illustrated / by Stephanie Wada ;
with translations by Gen P. Sakamoto.
p. cm.
ISBN 0-8076-1511-0 (hardcover)
1. Kuo'an, 12th cent. Shi niu tu song—Illustrations. 2. Spiritual life—Zen Buddhism.
I. Sakamoto, Gen P. II. Kuo'an, 12th cent. Shi niu tu song. English. III. Title.
BQ9288.K863 W33 2002
294.3'4432—dc21   2002074623

Photography credits:
Helmut Brinker, fig. 1; Otto E. Nelson, fig. 4; Carl Nardiello, fig. 6; and Bruce Schwarz, fig. 7
Color photography by Bruce Schwarz, courtesy of The Metropolitan Museum of Art.

Frontispiece: Scene Ten from the *Ten Oxherding Songs*

Design by Rita Lascaro
Printed and bound in Singapore by Tien Wah Press
First edition

Contents

Introduction

BY STEPHANIE WADA

The Buddha is just an old monk in the Western Heaven—
Is that something to look so hard for day and night?
It's you who are the Buddha, but you just won't see—
Why go riding on an ox to search for an ox?![1]
            —Wuxue Zuyuan (1226–1286)

When a person starts to search out the dharma [teachings of
the historical Buddha], he separates himself from the dharma.[2]
        —Dōgen (1200–1253), from the "Genjōkōan" chapter of
            the *Shōbōgenzō* (Treasury of the True Dharma Eye)

Traditional Buddhism was nearly a thousand years old when it was brought to Japan in the sixth century. Its origins lie in India, where it evolved from practices inspired by the life and teachings of Siddhartha (d. fifth century B.C.E.), also known by his family name of Gautama or as Shakyamuni, Sage of the Shakya Clan. Heir to the throne of a kingdom in the region of present-day Nepal, Shakyamuni abandoned palace life to search for a means by which to terminate human suffering. Through the practice of meditation he achieved supreme knowledge and became an enlightened being, or buddha. It became clear to him that the material world is illusory, that suffering is caused by desire, and that one can terminate suffering by ending one's attachment to the world and thus attain Nirvana (Sanskrit for "extinction"; Japanese: *nehan*)—freedom from earthly existence and escape from the endless cycle of life, death, and rebirth. For the remainder of his life Shakyamuni sought to teach others how to achieve this goal; after his death his beliefs were codified and spread by his followers.

Mahayana, the branch of Buddhism that eventually spread to Japan, recognized a large, hierarchically ranked pantheon of deities drawn from ancient Indian Vedic tradition, in addition to a multitude of buddhas and bodhisattvas (enlightened beings who choose to delay their entrance to Nirvana), and its prominent schools featured a vast canonical literature as well as complex rituals and icons of worship. It was formally introduced to the Japanese by emissaries from the kingdom of Paekche in southwest Korea, and within a century hundreds of temples had been constructed throughout Japan, presided over by more than a thousand clerics. During the Heian period (794–1185) a variety of Mahayana Buddhist sects flourished within the aristocratic circles that constituted Japan's educated elite. These traditional schools of Buddhism made use of a rich panoply of imagery drawn from sutras, sacred scriptures (from the Sanskrit: *sutra*); their temples employed sculptors, calligraphers, painters, and other artists and craftsmen to ornament interiors and the frontispieces of sutra handscrolls with figures of deities and scenes from Buddhist legend. Their rites and ceremonies served a social as well as a religious function, aimed at ensuring the well-being of the state and the rulers of the kingdom.

Zen (Chinese: Chan), which flourished in China from the Tang (618–906) through Song (960–1279) dynasty, became known to a small number of Japanese monks as early as the seventh century, but it was not until the end of the twelfth that the actual practice of Zen gained any measure of popularity in Japan. Zen (the name derives from the Sanskrit term *dhyana*, meaning "concentration" or "total immersion") was a school of Buddhism that developed in China, having been brought there, according to tradition, by the Indian patriarch Bodhidharma in the sixth century. In contrast to traditional Buddhist schools, whose priests encouraged the study of sacred writings and conducted complex or esoteric rituals in praise of or supplication to various deities, Zen was based on the concept of personal enlightenment (Japanese: *satori*) through meditation or direct and personal transmission from a master, without necessary recourse to scripture, ritual, or iconic images. Its emphasis on self-determination and self-discipline, combined with its basic pragmatism and absence of complicated practices, made it particularly appealing to the newly emerging Japanese military class of the Kamakura period (1185–1333), the samurai. These warriors, who had only just seized political control of the country from the imperial court and the aristocratic class, found the demands of Zen a refreshing alternative to classical Buddhist reliance on the reading and examination of religious texts. Zen, the meditation masters said, could not be "taught" in a traditional sense; enlightenment was an intuitive matter, a purely personal and individual experience attained through suppression of the individual ego and suspension of everyday modes of thought. Chinese Zen monks who emigrated to Japan, fleeing the Mongol occupation of their own country upon the fall of the Song dynasty, brought new and fascinating elements of continental culture to the Zen monasteries that sprang up in the Kamakura and Kyoto regions.

As Zen could not be taught through the methodical study of scriptures, and enlightenment was meant to be achieved as an intuitive rather than a logical process, Zen "instruction" often took the form of seemingly nonsensical riddles posed by a master to his pupil, or question-and-answer dialogues known as kōan (Japanese: *kōan*). These enigmatic exchanges were intended to liberate the mind from the binding and therefore self-defeating processes of intellectual and mundane thought, rendering it open and receptive to the sudden revelation of truth and realization of one's own Buddha nature: only then could transmission of a master's own meditation experiences take place. Another popular teaching method was the use of metaphors and allegories, which allowed the student of Zen to draw parallels between the progression of events in a tale and the various stages on the path to enlightenment.[3] Among these, one of the most popular was the theme of the Oxherder. This parable, best known as a series of poems entitled the *Ten Oxherding Songs,* compares the search of a herdboy for his missing ox to the individual's spiritual advance toward enlighten-ment. The ten stages in this quest to uncover the essential nature of things were fre-quently depicted in handscroll and hanging scroll paintings, with or without the corresponding verses. Most extant examples of Japanese "Oxherding Songs" paint-ings date to the latter half of the Muromachi period (1392–1573) or later, when artists executed these and other images of Zen themes in an ink brushwork style strongly influenced by Chinese ink painting.

An illustrated version of the oxherding parable owned by the Mary and Jackson Burke Foundation,[4] with alternating sections of painting and text inscribed in Chinese characters, is unique for several reasons. The inscription that concludes the final lines of calligraphy bears a reign date corresponding to the year 1278, making it the oldest known version of Japanese *Ten Oxherding Songs* paintings. Although mounted in the handscroll format—meant to be unrolled section by section and viewed from right to left—the narrow width of the joined sheets of paper suggests that its original form was that of a book with folded pages.[5] Most of the text with its cycle of ten four-line poems can be attributed to the twelfth-century Chinese Zen master Guoan Shiyuan, and his disciple Ciyuan, who composed the preface and the brief commentaries preceding each verse. An epilogue and single poem by the Japanese monk responsible for transcribing the text concludes the work. Unlike many early Japanese handscrolls and books, the Burke *Ten Oxherding Songs* is intact, from its preface explaining some basic tenets of Buddhism to its signed inscription. Moreover, the illustrations were painted not in the "Chinese style" but in the graceful, traditional manner of Japanese narrative illustration: the scenes of a youthful oxherder and his errant ox are simply rendered in fine ink outlines, delicate applications of color, and the inclusion of bucolic landscape elements that hint at the season of spring. These charming images render the message of the verses dou-bly appealing to the viewer, providing a visual record of how the mind can be freed from its attachment to the world of phenomena.

The Burke handscroll of the *Ten Oxherding Songs* was made during the Kamakura period, an era of political, social, and religious upheaval that began with the forcible transfer of power from the imperial family and aristocratic clans who had ruled Japan for many centuries to a recently risen warrior class. During the latter years of the preceding Heian period, while the courtier class enjoyed the elegant, cultured atmosphere of the capital city of Heian-kyō (Kyoto), administration of the provinces had been left in the hands of less highly placed, less privileged minor branches of noble families. In order to keep the peace in regions outside the charmed circle of Heian-kyō, provincial governors and the men they employed began to rely increasingly upon military prowess. The result was the development of a warrior class whose members patrolled and eventually gained control over the "frontier lands." These men—samurai—were totally unlike the refined, versifying aristocrats of the ruling elite; they placed more importance on fighting ability and military strategy than on training in the courtly arts. Two of the most powerful warrior clans, the Taira (or Heike) and Minamoto (or Genji), eventually faced each other in a bid for military supremacy that marked the close of the Heian period and the rise to prominence of samurai chieftains. Taira Kiyomori (1118–1181) was the first member of a military family to become ruler of Japan in all but name. His clan dominated the court and government until 1185 when, after several years of civil warfare, the Minamoto defeated Taira forces during a naval battle in the Inland Sea.

The head of the victorious clan, Minamoto Yoritomo (1147–1199), became Japan's first shogun, or military dictator (Japanese: *shōgun*), in 1192. He established his base of power in the small rural fishing community of Kamakura in eastern Honshu, the largest of the four principal islands of Japan, and set to work transforming it into the political center of a warrior government. With scenic mountains and hills on three sides and the beaches of Sagami Bay to the south, blessed by a mild climate, and a good three hundred miles from the imperial capital, Kamakura seemed the ideal place in which to keep members of a sober military administration removed from what Yoritomo saw as the corrupting influence of the old Kyoto aristocracy and its courtly traditions. The shogunate, or *bakufu,* ruled the country from eastern Japan, while the emperor and his circle, relegated to figurehead status, maintained their seat in Kyoto. Within roughly one hundred years Japan was run by a network of military governors and stewards appointed by the shogun. Changes in the economy encouraged the shogunate to look beyond national borders. Maritime trade with China, suspended in the late ninth century (except for the activities of privateers in Kyūshū), had been renewed in the late twelfth. Although commercial exchange between the two countries was interrupted again in 1274 and 1281, when Mongol leader Khubilai Khan (r. 1260–94) launched two failed attempts to invade Japan, trade was resumed again before the close of the thirteenth century. In the meantime, one significant side effect of Mongol expansionism was the flight of Chinese Zen Buddhist monks to the relative safety of Japan.

Chinese Zen refugees found that the religious climate of early Kamakura-period Japan was one of reform, evangelism, revivalism, and openness toward new concepts. For the first time, various forms of Buddhism were being brought within reach of the common people, spread through the provinces by proselytizing monks and their enthusiastic followers. The old Nara sects that had dominated Japan in earlier times were revived. New salvationist movements like the Pure Land and Nichiren sects found wide audiences through their emphasis on achieving an enlightened state through faith alone. Unlike these indigenous sects, which advocated complete faith in something outside and beyond the human realm—the saving power of buddhas or bodhisattvas, for instance—Zen Buddhism took a firm stance against the idea that enlightenment or Buddhahood could be sought outside of oneself.[6] Zen placed importance upon individual effort and discipline rather than simple belief, but its directness, and its aim of awakening the Buddha nature that lies within every person, rendered it attractive. Not long after the Rinzai (Chinese: Linji) and Sōtō (Chinese: Caodong) branches of Zen were brought to Japan from China in the late twelfth and early thirteenth centuries, respectively, members of the samurai elite seized upon Zen as a form of Buddhism well suited to the austerity and stoicism of the warrior code. To the shoguns it had the added appeal of a recently imported faith with no connection to the old courtier class; they appreciated it also as a conduit to the learning and literary-artistic traditions of China. These new Chinese influences, they believed, would help them elevate the cultural environment of Kamakura without recourse to the aristocratic habits of Kyoto.

Although uncouth and provincial by court standards, some of the newly powerful samurai lords were astute men with inquiring minds who sought to bolster their image as legitimate leaders. In spite of shogunal injunctions to safeguard the disciplined, spartan samurai lifestyle, they had already begun to adopt certain courtly customs, such as the holding of poetry competitions. They viewed the new continental knowledge, coupled with the self-reliance of Zen, as a means of enhancing both their status and their political power. The Hōjō clan, who gained control of the military government after Yoritomo's death, became active lay practitioners and sponsors of Zen, commissioning the construction of temple monasteries and inviting Chinese monks to settle in Japan as teachers and abbots of the new Zen centers. The Hōjō Regents, as they were called, and their vassals, were particularly enthusiastic in their devotion to this "new" meditational Buddhism, and their material support facilitated the spread of Zen throughout the country. They and other wealthy daimyo (warlords) began to collect Chinese works of art and encourage the study and copying of Chinese texts. The Chinese Zen masters who found a haven in Japan after Mongol persecution were often men of learning, accomplished painters, poets, and even architects, who were pleased to instruct Japanese warrior chieftains in cultural as well as spiritual pursuits. Likewise, Japanese monks who risked the treacherous sea voyage to study on the continent returned with examples of Chinese calligraphy, portraits of the masters with whom they had practiced, and paintings produced by literati as well as monk-artists, all of which fascinated warlord collectors and became influential in the formation of the new daimyo culture.

Foremost among the Japanese Zen teachers of the thirteenth century were Eisai (1141–1215), regarded as the founder of Rinzai Zen in Japan, and the severe Dōgen (1200–1253), who introduced Sōtō Zen. Both men studied in China with Zen masters and both, upon returning to their homeland, became active and influential in Kyoto and Kamakura. Among the Chinese Zen masters who settled in Japan and found favor with the Hōjō Regents and other daimyo were Lanqi Daolong (1213–1278, known in Japan as Rankei Dōryū), Yishan Yining (Issan Ichinei, 1247–1317), and Wuxue Zuyuan (Mugaku Sogen, 1226–1286). Lanqi Daolong became founding abbot of the great temple-monastery of Kenchōji in Kamakura; the scholarly Yishan Yining, third abbot of Nanzenji in Kyoto, was in large part responsible for the florescence of Chinese culture in both the old capital and the new shogunal city; while Wuxue Zuyuan was made first abbot of Engakuji, second of the great Kamakura Zen temples. Wuxue Zuyuan, who had fled China under pain of execution by the Mongol invaders, received an especially warm welcome from Hōjō Tokimune (1251–1284), to whom he became a friend as well as mentor. As a senior prelate of Rinzai Zen he gave instruction to both monk disciples and lay followers, and apart from introducing the way of Zen to the more educated members of Kamakura warrior society, he was instrumental in making the contemporary style of Chinese calligraphy known to the Japanese.[7]

The making of the Burke *Ten Oxherding Songs* handscroll more or less coincided with several noteworthy events in the early history of Chinese studies and Zen Buddhism in Japan. The first was the founding in 1275 of the Kanazawa Bunko, a library of Chinese books, by Hōjō Sanetoki (1225–1276), grandson of one of the Hōjō Regents; this became one of the most important centers of learning in the country. The next event, in the very year in which the Burke handscroll was produced, was the death of Lanqi Daolong, first of the transplanted Chinese abbots to establish contemporary Chinese Zen practices and regulations within a Japanese monastery. The third, a year later, was the arrival in Japan of Wuxue Zuyuan, whose method of instruction helped to popularize parables already known in some Japanese Zen circles. The use of kōan and allegory was a primary teaching vehicle of the Rinzai sect of Zen (Sōtō Zen placed far greater emphasis upon *zazen,* or seated meditation), and one of the Chinese parables Wuxue Zuyuan utilized to explain the individual's search for enlightenment was that of the oxherder and the missing ox. His words, "It's you who are the Buddha, but you just won't see—/Why go riding on an ox to search for an ox?!" are a clear reference to the theme of the *Ten Oxherding Songs,* with the ox as a symbol of the Buddha nature within every living thing.

THE TEN OXHERDING SONGS

The Zen parable set forth in the *Ten Oxherding Songs* became a popular instructional vehicle in the Rinzai Zen monasteries of the Kamakura period for several reasons. Unlike kōan, which were, when initially encountered, completely senseless in nature, the *Oxherding Song*s possessed a narrative quality that rendered them accessible to the new Zen practitioner or lay follower. That the analogy made between the oxherder's search and the achievement of enlightenment was offered in steps or stages—representing degrees of enlightenment or preparation for enlightenment— made the path to satori appear less daunting. When presented in illustrated form, the parable became a visual as well as written guide to the process by which one could subdue and ultimately "forget" the self, lose attachment to the material world, and become one with one's Buddha nature.

Although Japanese Zen monks of the thirteenth century naturally associated the creation of the oxherding parable with Chinese Song-dynasty meditation masters, including the author of the verses in the Burke handscroll, the Rinzai Zen priest Guoan Shiyuan (active ca. 1150), they probably had little knowledge of the theme's ancient roots in early, pre-Zen Buddhist writings. In India, where the long-standing sacred status of the bull may have contributed to the animal's frequent appearance in legends of other Asian countries, the concept behind the oxherding theme can be traced to an early sutra comparing the herding of cattle to the responsibilities of a

Buddhist monk.[8] However, the specific imagery found in the *Ten Oxherding Songs* certainly evolved in China, where before the advent of Zen the image of the ox (or water buffalo or bull) had religious significance as a fertility symbol,[9] associated with agriculture and the prevention of floods and other natural disasters.[10] In Daoist philosophy, the ox and herdboy were emblematic of the seasonal rhythms of nature and the pleasures of bucolic country life. Chinese literature and painting abounded with depictions of gentleman-scholars and Daoist sages riding on the backs of placid oxen. During the Song dynasty, scenes of a young herdboy and his beast (or beasts) in gentle landscape surroundings were frequently produced by academic court painters. These peaceful genre pictures, usually set in the spring season—a symbol of renewal—were inspired by Daoist thought, but it was also about this time that the Zen version of the ox and herdboy theme began to appear in Zen painting.

The origins of the fully fledged ox and oxherder parable can be traced to the Tang dynasty, at least as far back as the ninth century. According to the writings of the Song-dynasty Zen master Dachuan Puji (1179–1253), an exchange between the master Baizheng Huaihai (720–814) and his disciple began with the question of how to search for the Buddha without knowing the way. The master's response: "It is as if one were looking for an ox on which one is riding."[11] When the pupil asked what he was to do after becoming conscious of the truth, the master replied, "It is like returning home on the back of an ox."[12] By the mid-eleventh century, sets of allegorical poems on the subject of the oxherder as a seeker of truth had been composed and grouped together to form models for subsequent recensions. One set, by the eleventh-century (?) master Dabai Puming, contained ten poems, while another similar grouping by a Master Qingjiu contained twelve.[13] The ten-poem version by Guoan Shiyuan was published in woodblock-printed form; this set of verses, with accompanying illustrations, was introduced to Japan during the early decades of the Kamakura period.[14] Guoan's *Oxherding Songs* and their accompanying preface by Guoan's disciple, Ciyuan, became widely known in Japanese Zen circles, their popularity ensured by the copying and reprinting of the Chinese text. The titles and basic content of the poems describe the seeker's movement or progression toward enlightenment that the pictorial scenes in illustrated versions were meant to reinforce.

1. SEARCHING FOR THE OX

A herdboy and the ox in his charge have become separated. The boy sets out to find the animal but is confused by the intersecting mountain paths. Far from home and exhausted from his efforts, he is assailed by feelings of doubt.

2. SEEING THE FOOTPRINTS OF THE OX

Having read the sutras and grasped their content, the boy notices traces of the missing ox. He recognizes the unity of all things, yet still cannot distinguish truth from falsehood.

3. SEEING THE OX

Upon hearing the sound of the ox, the herdboy sets off to recover what he has lost. When all of his senses work together, his eyes are opened and he catches his first glimpse of the ox's majestic horned head.

4. CATCHING THE OX

The ox has been alone in the field for so long that it has become quite wild. It longs for the fragrant grass around it and is difficult to catch. The boy catches hold of it, but it is stubborn and resists. If he wishes to tame the creature, the boy cannot give up; he must use the whip and persevere.

5. HERDING THE OX

When he holds the nose-rope tightly, the ox is finally calmed. By keeping a firm grip on the rope, the boy is able to control him. He realizes that delusion is something that originates within himself, not in the world around him.

6. RIDING THE OX AND RETURNING HOME

Having finally tamed the ox, the boy rides homeward, playing children's tunes on his flute. His mind is now clear and he does not look back.

7. THE OX FORGOTTEN, THE MAN REMAINS

The boy is back at home, but the ox is no longer seen. Since the boy now sees the truth (or has become enlightened), he no longer needs what he was searching for, and he is at ease, all confusion gone.

8. THE OX AND THE MAN, BOTH FORGOTTEN

Both the ox and oxherd have vanished; emptiness remains. All attachment to "self" and to earthly things has gone, and praise is meaningless.

9. RETURN TO THE FUNDAMENTALS, BACK TO THE SOURCE

The waters of the earth are blue, the mountains green, flowers red. Having transcended all aspects of the physical world, one can observe that world from the vantage point of nonbeing.

10. ENTERING THE CITY WITH HANDS HANGING DOWN

The herdboy reappears in the form of Hotei (Chinese: Budai), the bald, rotund, sack-toting reincarnation of Miroku (Sanskrit: Maitreya), the Buddha of the Future. Although his actions seem mundane (going to the market, returning home), he is an enlightened being. (In the Burke *Ten Oxherding Songs*, Hotei is depicted alone; in some versions he appears with the oxherd.)

In his preface to the poems, Ciyuan cites the very first instance of Zen transmission of the dharma (Buddhist Law), which occurred when Shakyamuni winked or blinked his eyes and thus wordlessly conveyed his teaching "and the Serene Mind of Nirvana" to his disciple Mahakasyapa.[15] Ciyuan then explains how enlightenment can save all sentient beings from the cycle of rebirth and why the historical Buddha, Shakyamuni, was compassionate enough to offer a variety of paths to Buddhahood. In accordance with this variety, Ciyuan continues, a Chinese master of Chan (Zen) Buddhism created the oxherding parable "and taught it according to varying circumstances." In Ciyuan's words, Guoan's own verses on the subject were "created from

[his] own heart," corresponding to the different needs of different people, "like giving food to the hungry and water to the thirsty."

The final section of the Burke handscroll contains a postscript by an unknown Japanese monk whose abbreviated signature (in the form of a *kaō*, or personalized cipher) can only be read in part as "—gi" (possibly "Kōgi").[16] It offers the monk's own poem on the subject of the ox and herdboy, a kind of grace note to Guoan's set of verses.

As well known as Guoan's *Ten Oxherding Songs* became in Japan, it enjoyed only limited popularity among the Chinese. In China a version of the parable utilizing the imagery of Puming and Qingjiu's *Oxherding Songs*[17] became a subject for Zen artists. This approach, a simplified metaphor for the progression toward enlightenment, depicted an ox whose color turned from ink-black to white before the animal finally became invisible. The last stage of this cycle was represented by an empty circle, symbol of non-existence or the unity of opposites and differences within the ultimate truth of satori.

The appearance of an ox as focal point of a Zen parable may have held some appeal to the Japanese, as bulls and oxen had figured in Japan's native Shinto and traditional Buddhist legends prior to the spread of Zen. Tenjin, the Shinto patron god of scholarship (the posthumously deified minister Sugawara Michizane [ca. 840–903]), was closely associated with the ox, a sculpture of which adorns the compound of his shrine in Kyoto, the Kitano Tenmangu. The multilimbed, six-headed Daiitoku Myōō, a deity of Esoteric Buddhism, was commonly depicted astride a bull or water buffalo. In stories surrounding the founding and restoration of the seventh-century Buddhist temple Jin'oji in Osaka, a Korean monk was guided to the ruins of the temple by the mysterious figure of a bull.[18] On an even more fantastic note was the tale of a "Buddha-ox" recorded in the *Konjaku monogatari* (Tales of Times Now Past), a collection of more than twelve hundred stories on an extremely broad variety of subjects, secular and religious, assembled during the twelfth century. According to this account, a black ox employed to haul building materials at the temple of Sekidera suddenly proclaimed itself "the Buddha Kashō," come to "help the temple and spread the holy Teaching." [19] Many came to worship at the stable of the amazing ox, including a lord chancellor of the imperial court, who in his eagerness drove his carriage straight up to the ox's stall. The deity "seemed deeply offended by this sacrilege because it suddenly broke its tether and bolted for the hills. The chancellor . . . burst into tears at the thought that his conduct had displeased the ox and made it run away." [20]

THE BURKE HANDSCROLL AND THE LINEAGE OF JAPANESE OXHERDING PAINTINGS

Given the Japanese fondness for tales—religious and secular—combining the theme of a search (or unraveling of a mystery) with a strong element of human emotion, it was inevitable that linked allegorical verses like the *Ten Oxherding Songs* found favor in Zen circles as a subject for painting. The presence in Japan of a Chinese model with wood-block illustrations must have made the prospect of creating their own versions irresistible to artists, among whom the copying of pictures from newly imported Chinese books may have become something of a fashion. [21] To painters of narrative illustration, stories involving a search or movement from one location to another were well suited to the handscroll design, whose horizontally oriented surface gave the viewer a sense of the passage of time as the scroll was unrolled on the left side and simultaneously rolled up on the right, so that a portion only about twenty to twenty-four inches (fifty to sixty centimeters) wide was exposed at once. Although less cinematic in overall effect, the illustrated book format with folded pages, in which the Burke *Ten Oxherding Songs* was originally rendered, also provided a feeling of the progression of events or movement toward an unknown future; the folded pages could even be spread out for a handscroll-like effect.

As the *Oxherding Songs* consisted of ten distinct episodes, it was logical that each episode should have been represented by one image. Sets of ten pictures became the norm, although single paintings depicting one stage in the parable alone were also created. The paintings sometimes included the poems, though by the fifteenth century the parable was so well known that accompanying text was not necessary.

In Japan, Zen painting is inextricably associated with ink painting styles influenced by Chinese brushwork of the Song (960–1279) and Yuan (1260–1368) dynasties. The emphasis in Zen upon simplicity and spontaneity made ink monochrome a suitable medium for artistic expression. Although until the sixteenth century most ink painters who produced works on Zen themes were monks, contrary to popular belief not all such paintings were executed as a spiritual exercise or an extension of the meditation and discipline that were part of the rigorous monastic lifestyle. Many were painted for friends and associates, or even pro-duced on commission. The Chinese models that served as their inspiration were treasured in temple and daimyo collections. In addition to the Chinese

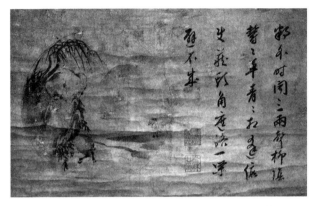

FIGURE 1. "Seeing the Ox" from the *Ten Oxherding Parable*, inscription by Shaolin Miaosong (active first half of the thirteenth century), hanging scroll, Southern Song dynasty (1185–1279), Yabumoto Kōzō Collection, Amagasaki

printed renditions of Guoan Shiyuan's *Ten Oxherding Songs,* some actual Song-dynasty paintings on the theme may have been present in Japan as early as the first half of the thirteenth century. One small hanging scroll in the collection of Yabumoto Kōzō in Japan (fig. 1),[22] painted in an abbreviated manner in ink with fluid, wet brushstrokes and soft washes, and inscribed by the Chinese monk Shaolin Miaosong (late twelfth–early thir-teenth century), may represent the type of Chinese oxherding painting to which the Japanese were first exposed.

A classic example of Japanese *Ten Oxherding Songs* painting, a handscroll belong-ing to Shōkokuji temple in Kyoto (fig. 2), exhibits composition and brushwork that clearly derived from Chinese ink landscape and figure painting, although in a crisp, linear style more closely related to works of the Southern Song (1185–1279) court painting academy than the soft "splashed-ink" technique of the Yabumoto hanging scroll. This work, except

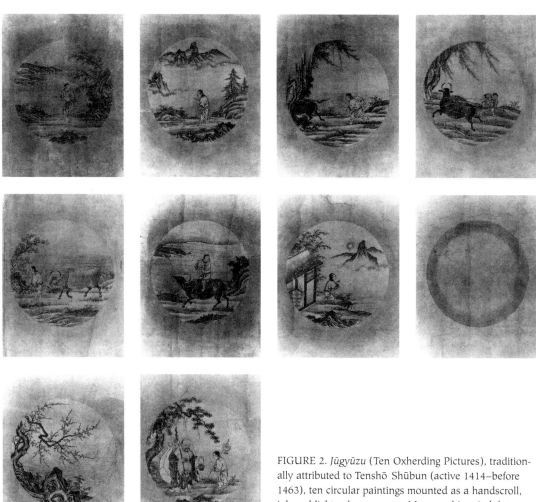

FIGURE 2. *Jūgyūzu* (Ten Oxherding Pictures), traditionally attributed to Tenshō Shūbun (active 1414–before
1463), ten circular paintings mounted as a handscroll,
ink and light color on paper, Muromachi period, late
fifteenth century, 12⅝ x 71⁷/₁₆ in. (32 x 181.5 cm),
Shōkokuji temple, Kyoto

for the Burke handscroll the earliest-known example of Japanese *Ten Oxherding* painting,
is attributed traditionally to the great ink painter Tenshō Shūbun (active 1414–before
1463). Though almost certainly not from that master's hand, it appears to be a genuine
late fifteenth-century work painted by a well-trained and highly skilled artist. The handscroll, essentially a series of ten circular ink paintings with mere touches of light color,
mounted in the handscroll format, contains no text. In the scenes a childlike herdboy, his
garments delineated with dark strokes terminating in the angular hooks and "nailheads"

of Chinese-style brushwork, seeks his ox in landscape settings evocative of academy-painted landscapes of the Southern Song: craggy mountain peaks rise from the mist, trees are bent and twisted angular shapes with stabbing, zigzag branches crossing the picture plane at a diagonal, rendered with strong dark outlines. Scenes Three, Seven, Nine, and Ten also display the type of composition commonly associated with Southern Song academy artists like Ma Yuan (active ca. 1190–1225), with most foreground elements restricted to one side of the painting surface, an invisible diagonal line dividing the image into filled and relatively empty space. Sharply defined foreground rocks and overlapping planes on the cliff face of Scenes One and Three are reminiscent of the work of Ma Yuan's contemporary, the academy painter Xia Gui (active ca. 1195–1230).

The use of circular frames to separate the illustrations of the *Ten Oxherding Songs* originated with the Chinese versions of the theme.[23] It was an effective and visually pleasing means of conveying the significance of each of the steps described in the oxherding poems, as well as a reference to the symbolic circle of the eighth scene. A handscroll in the Spencer Collection of the New York Public Library, produced about a hundred years later than the Shōkokuji version, follows a similar layout, although the scenes are enclosed within fan-shaped borders that occasionally overlap in a decorative manner to create the impression of scattered fan-paintings (fig. 3). This

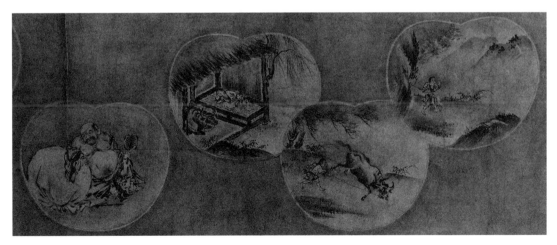

FIGURE 3. Section of *Jūgyūzu* (Ten Oxherding Pictures), handscroll, ink on paper, Momoyama period, sixteenth century, 9¹/₂ x 43¹¹/₁₆ in. (24.2 x 111 cm), Spencer Collection, The New York Public Library

FIGURE 4. *Ox and Herdboy*, by Sekkyakushi (fl. first half of the fifteenth century), hanging scroll, ink on paper, Muromachi period, 21¹⁄₈ x 11⁵⁄₈ in. (53.6 x 29.6 cm), property of Mary Griggs Burke

Momoyama-period (1573–1615) work, painted in ink monochrome with a combination of calligraphic, modulated brushstrokes and wash, was in all likelihood made by an artist outside of the temple milieu rather than a monk-painter (hence its incorrect sequence of episodes and the inclusion of the ox in Scene Seven). Nevertheless, it is indisputably similar in type to the Shōkokuji scroll.

Episodes from the *Ten Oxherding Songs* were also illustrated independent of each other or in sets of hanging scrolls that could be displayed separately or together. From about the first half of the fourteenth century the hanging scroll—a larger, less intimate format for painting than the handscroll—was a popular vehicle for oxherding pictures. These larger-scale ink monochrome compositions were of course influenced by Chinese hanging-scroll paintings that had found their way into Japan.[24] One example painted by the early-fifteenth-century artist Sekkyakushi (fig. 4) in the collection of Mary Griggs Burke represents the fifth episode from the *Ten Oxherding Songs* and features the simple arrangement of pictorial motifs and expressive use of ink that had become hallmarks of Zen painters. More monumental in design than the small-book or handscroll images, such pictures could also be hung in monastery interiors or private homes to provide instruction or inspiration to the monk or lay practitioner. In keeping with Zen practice, they never served the function of iconic images for worship in the manner of orthodox Buddhism.

Because of the widespread popularity of the oxherding theme, depictions of the oxherder and his ox began to appear as decorative motifs on works of art and craft outside of the monastic and temple environment. The herdboy playing his flute while reclining on the haunches of his strolling ox—a reference to the sixth of the *Ten Oxherding Songs*—decorates the lid of a Muromachi-period ovoid lacquer box also in the collection of Mary Griggs Burke (fig. 5). The image, executed in sprinkled gold powder on the gleaming black lacquer surface, serves an ornamental function to which the spiritual message now appears secondary. During the Edo period (1615–1868) the design of objects made for practical use like incense burners and netsuke (small, carved toggles of wood or ivory used to secure the cord of a purse or seal case suspended from a sash) utilized the ox and herdboy motif. A bronze incense burner in the shape of the ox, the lid consisting of the seated figure of the oxherder, his hair fastened into the two small side knots worn by young Chinese boys (fig. 6, also in the collection of Mary Griggs Burke), is a charming example of this type of functional art.

FIGURE 5. Lidded black lacquer box with sprinkled gold design of herdboy and ox, Muromachi period (1392–1573), 6⁷/₈ x 4⁷/₁₆ in. (17.4 x 11.2 cm), property of Mary Griggs Burke

As the earliest known rendition of *Ten Oxherding Songs* illustrations painted in Japan, the Burke handscroll derived its compositional elements as well as most of its text from the Chinese models to which the above-mentioned paintings owe their basic inspiration. However, one of the most striking characteristics of the Burke scroll is the style in which its small, roundel-enclosed scenes were executed. It is an unmistakable synthesis of Chinese pictorial motifs and stylistic elements drawn from the modes of narrative painting practiced by artists of twelfth- and

FIGURE 6. Incense burner in the shape of a Chinese herdboy and ox, bronze, Edo period (1615–1868), H. 5¹/₄ in. (13.4 cm), property of Mary Griggs Burke

FIGURE 7. Scene Three from the *Jūgyūzu* (Ten Oxherding Songs), handscroll, ink and color on paper, Kamakura period, 1278, 1 ft. ¹/₄ in. x 20 ft. 6 in. (31 x 624.6 cm), Mary and Jackson Burke Foundation

FIGURE 8. One of the *Semmen Hoke-kyō* (Lotus Sutra text printed on Fan-shaped Booklets), fan-shaped paper, ink, color, and gold on paper, Heian period, twelfth century, 37⁵/₈ x 19⁷/₁₆ in. (95.6 x 49.4 cm), Shitennōji temple, Osaka

thirteenth-century Japan for their renditions of native *monogatari* ("tales" or "stories") and *setsuwa* (shorter narratives collected into compilations). Even though the oxherder is given the garb and hairstyle of a Chinese boy, and Hotei is drawn in accordance with his Chinese iconography, the abbreviated landscapes eschew the stony mountains and rugged cliff faces of Chinese ink painting. Instead, the landscape components in the various scenes—hills, rocks, grasses, and banks of earth delineated with soft, curving brush-strokes—parallel details found in many Japanese *emaki* (illustrated handscrolls) of the late Heian and early Kamakura periods. The relatively uninflected outlines and use of bright but transparent colors are typical of a number of twelfth-century handscrolls like the famous *Shigisan engi emaki* (Scroll of the History of Mount Shigi) in the collection of Chōgosonshiji temple in Nara and the thirteenth-century *Kegon engi emaki* (Illustrated Scroll of the Patriarchs of Kegon Buddhism), in Kōzanji, Kyoto. The sinuous trees with bifurcated, crisscrossing trunks in Scenes Two and Three (fig. 7) are of a type that appears repeatedly in narrative illustration: some of the best-known examples include the twelfth-century *Chōjū jinbutsu giga-kan* (Scroll of Frolicking Animals and Humans, also in the Kōzanji collection), the thirteenth-century *Saigyō monogatari emaki*

(Illustrated Biography of the Monk Saigyō) in the Tokugawa Art Museum, Nagoya, and the Man'no Art Museum, Osaka, and Buddhist works like the twelfth-century fan-shaped album leaves (fig. 8) with text from the Lotus Sutra printed over landscape or narrative scenes (in the collection of Shitennōji temple, Osaka). The trunk of the gnarled plum tree in Scene Nine of the Burke *Ten Oxherding Songs* is split by a dark band of ink that makes it appear to be hollowed out, a device that occurs more than once in the

Saigyō monogatari emaki (fig. 9). Even the intimacy with minute aspects of nature, like birdsong, mist, and wildflowers, that pervades much of classical Japanese illustration appears here in tiny details like the bird perched on a willow tree in Scene Three. This is a reference to the poem, which describes a bush warbler singing on a branch; the bird does not appear in the famous ink-monochrome version of Shōkokuji.

The inclusion of genre elements—ordinary, homely objects unrelated to the text of the poems—in Scene Seven of the Burke scroll is reminiscent of similar details in late-Heian-period handscrolls like the *Shigisan engi emaki* noted above. The herdboy is shown sitting pensively

FIGURE 9. Detail from *Saigyō monogatari emaki* (Illustrated Biography of the Monk Saigyō), handscroll, ink and color on paper, Kamakura period, thirteenth century, 11¹⁵/₁₆ in. x 37 ft. 2⅝ in. (30.3 x 1134.4 cm), Man'no Art Museum, Osaka

outside his rustic hut near an undulating shoreline, the red disk of the sun above. His whip and rope, both mentioned in the poem, have been placed on the ground beside him. However, the hat of woven grass or straw and the straw rain cape, of the type worn by commoners,[25] that lie close by have no relevance to the text. In a secular genre scene they would have been added as indications of a herdboy's humble social status; here they are charming motifs used to emphasize the rural nature of the boy's surroundings. Paradoxically, the herdboy's Chinese dress is somewhat more elegant than the peasant garb commonly depicted in later ink-painting versions of the theme; his two tidy knots of hair, vermillion tunic over a green shirt, trousers, and black shoes contrast with the simpler tunic and trousers, loose hair, and bare feet of the figures in the Shōkokuji and New York Public Library paintings.

Finally, the ox itself, defined by even outlines and fine ink brushstrokes on the head and body, is reminiscent of the prized bulls depicted in thirteenth-century paintings entitled *Shungyū zu* (Pictures of Excellent Bulls).[26] These bull "portraits," which became fashionable about the thirteenth century, preserved images of the powerful oxen used to draw the curtained and decorated carriages of the nobility in the old capital city. A portion of one of these handscrolls in the Cleveland Museum of Art (fig. 10)[27] displays a robust creature with the short legs and muscular but rounded body that characterize the ox in the Burke handscroll. Scenes of these handsome animals and carriages making their sedate way along the avenues (where they were frequently the cause of the worst traffic gridlock) appear in paintings like the thirteenth-century *Komakurabe gyoko emaki* (Handscroll of an Imperial Visit to the Horse Race) in the Kubōsō Memorial Museum of Arts, Izumi. Artists of the time must have become accustomed to producing images of bulls, which were also not uncommon in traditional Buddhist paintings like *nehan zu*—pictures of the Nirvana, or "death" of the historical Buddha—in which the reclining Shakyamuni is surrounded by disciples, supernatural beings, and animals. The half-hidden ox in Scene Four of the Burke handscroll recalls the reclining oxen depicted in more than one *nehan* painting of the era.[28]

Why the unknown artist of the Burke *Ten Oxherding Songs* illustrations decided, or was instructed, to take the essential figures and motifs from the Chinese model and execute them in an indigenous style of painting may have had more to do with a desire for visual appeal than the actual content of the *Oxherding Songs*. By the late thirteenth century, Japanese Zen monk-artists were still struggling with the more sophisticated nuances of Chinese ink painting techniques, but they were well enough versed in the medium that it did not seem alien or lacking in aesthetic value. On the other hand the storylike qual-

FIGURE 10. *One of Ten Fast Bulls*, section of a handscroll mounted as a hanging scroll, ink and slight color on paper, Kamakura period, thirteenth century, 10³/₄ x 12⁵/₈ in. (27.3 x 32 cm), The Cleveland Museum of Art, John L. Severance Fund, 1952.286

ity of the *Ten Oxherding Songs,* with its distinct progression of events, must have seemed to the artist, scribe, and possible patron involved in the project to be ideally suited to the conventions of their own narrative painting. Perhaps they wished to offer the metaphor of the ox and oxherder in such a way that it was couched—at least on a visual level— in familiar terms. The gentle, unthreatening hints of scenic native vistas in the Burke handscroll endow the images with a feeling that is benign rather than anticipatory, reassuring rather than startling. The only scene that implies a sense of agitation is the image representing Poem Four, "Catching the Ox," in which writhing, scudding clouds more closely resemble the curling cloud scrolls found in some Song-dynasty landscape and Buddhist paintings than the flat bands of mist characteristic of Japanese *emaki.*

While the overall impression of serenity may not have been the atmosphere that later Zen monks sought in their words or paintings—their goal, after all, was to jolt pupils out of their habitual, rational mode of perception—in the thirteenth century it made for a comforting interpretation of a "new" type of subject matter. Zen encouraged its followers to break all ties with worldly considerations in order to achieve a truth that is beyond words, obtainable as transmission from master to pupil or in the quiet of solitary meditation, yet it never denied the inspiring role that the literary and visual arts could play in the monastic environment. The creators of the Burke *Ten Oxherding Songs* might have reasoned thus: by enabling followers to view the pictures with pleasure and emotional involvement, they were rendering them (contradictory as it might seem) more receptive to the message contained therein.

1. David Pollack, *Zen Poems of the Five Mountains,* Studies in Religion, no. 37 (New York and Decatur, Ga.: American Academy of Religion, 1985), 25.

2. Hakuun Yasutari, *Flowers Fall: A Commentary on Dōgen's Genjōkōan,* trans. Paul Jaffe (Boston and London: Shambhala Publications, Inc., 1996), 42.

3. Zen allegories, parables, and *zenkizu* (parable paintings) are examined in Helmut Brinker and Hiroshi Kanazawa, *Zen: Masters of Meditation in Images and Writings,* trans. Andreas Leisinger, Supplementum, no. 40 (Zurich: Artibus Asiae Publishers, 1996), 169–78.

4. Published in Miyeko Murase, *Bridge of Dreams: The Mary Griggs Burke Collection of Japanese Art* (New York: The Metropolitan Museum of Art, 2000), 114–17; Ebine Toshio, *Suibokuga: Mokuan kara Minchō e* (Ink Painting: From Mokuan to Minchō), Nihon no bijutsu, no. 333 (Tokyo: Shibundō, 1994), fig. 31(c); Shinbo Tōru, "Shinshutsu no Kōanbon Jūgyū zukan: Sorimachi Jūrō shi zō" (Recently Discovered Paintings of Zen Enlightenment: The Kōan Scroll of Ten Oxherding Pictures in the Sorimachi Collection), *Bukkyō geijutsu,* no. 96 (May 1974): 77–79.

5. Murase, *Bridge of Dreams,* 115.

6. See William Theodore de Bary, *The Buddhist Tradition in India, China, and Japan* (New York: Vintage Books, 1972), 355.

7. This style of writing can be seen in a letter he wrote to Hojō Tokimune in 1282. See Yoshiaki Shimizu, *Japan: The Shaping of Daimyo Culture 1185–1868* (Washington: National Gallery of Art, 1988), 106.

8. The *Ekottaragama sutra;* see Brinker and Kanazawa, *Zen: Masters of Meditation,* 172; and Daisetz T. Suzuki, *Essays in Zen Buddhism,* first series (London, 1927), 355.

9. Miyeko Murase et al., *Jewel Rivers: Japanese Art from the Burke Collection* (Richmond: Virginia Museum of Fine Arts, 1993), 54.

10. Wai-kam Ho et al., *Eight Dynasties of Chinese Painting: The Collections of the Nelson Gallery-Atkins Museum, Kansas City, and the Cleveland Museum of Art* (Cleveland: The Cleveland Museum of Art, 1980), 57.

11. Brinker and Kanazawa, *Zen: Masters of Meditation,* 170.

12. Ibid.

13. Ueda Shizuteru and Yanagida Seizan, *Jūgyūzū* (Ten Oxherding Pictures), (Tokyo, 1992), 273.

14. Murase, *Bridge of Dreams,* 114.

15. See also the discussion of early Zen literature, specifically works by Dōgen, in Donald Keene, *Seeds in the Heart: Japanese Literature from Earliest Times to the Late Sixteenth Century* (New York: Henry Holt and Company, 1993), 757.

16. Murase, *Bridge of Dreams,* 115.

17. Ueda and Yanagida, *Jūgyūzu,* 273–74.

18. The legends of the founding of Jin'ōji were illustrated in the handscroll format during the fourteenth century. Portions of this *Jin'ōji engi emaki* (Handscroll of the History of Jin'ōji) are divided among a number of collections; the scene depicting the miraculous (green) bull is in the Avery Brundage Collection, the Asian Art Museum of San Francisco. See Akiyama Terukazu, "Jin'ōji engi emaki no fukugen to kōsatsu: Iwayuru Kōnin Shōnin eden o megutte" (The Reconstruction and Examination of the Illustrated History of Jin'ōji: Regarding the Illustrated Biography of the Monk Kōnin), in Akiyama Terukazu, ed., *Emakimono* (Illustrated Handscrolls), Zaigai Nihon no shihō (Selections of Japanese Art in Western Collections), vol. 2 (Tokyo: Mainichi Shimbunsha, 1980), 98–113.

19. Translated in Royall Tyler, *Japanese Tales* (New York: Pantheon Books, 1987), 287–89.

20. Ibid.

21. Murase, *Bridge of Dreams,* 115.

22. The painting is one of four extant scenes (one of which is a later copy) from a set, now dispersed. See Brinker and Kanazawa, *Zen: Masters of Meditation*, 171–72.

23. Later Japanese woodblock-printed book versions of the *Ten Oxherding Songs* preserved this format, placing the illustrations within roundels that were sometimes separated by text. An example dated 1419 (in a private collection in Japan), and another, dated 1620 (in the Spencer Collection of the New York Public Library), follow this design. See Mosaku Ishida et al., *Japanese Buddhist Prints* (New York: Harry N. Abrams, Inc., and Kodansha International Ltd., 1964), fig. 159; and Murase, *Bridge of Dreams*, 114, fig. 29.

24. For Chinese hanging-scroll paintings of oxen and herdboys, see examples published in Toda Teisuke, ed., *Mokkei, Gyokukan* (Muqi and Yujian), vol. 3, Suiboku bijutsu taikei (Tokyo: Kodansha, 1973).

25. Rain capes of the common people were generally made from stalks of straw, sedge, or miscanthus grass. Aristocrats wore rain gear made of water-repellent oiled silk.

26. Murase, *Bridge of Dreams*, 115; these "bull portraits" are discussed in Miyeko Murase, *Court and Samurai in an Age of Transition: Medieval Paintings and Blades from the Gotoh Museum, Tokyo* (New York: Japan Society, 1990), 46–47.

27. See Akiyama Terukazu, ed., *Emakimono*, 146, pl. 48.

28. Several Kamakura-period Nirvana paintings depict an ox (or water buffalo) in a reclining pose, its head turned away from the viewer. A thirteenth-century hanging-scroll Nirvana close in date (1274) to the Burke *Ten Oxherding Songs* is a good example; see *Buddha Shakuson: Sono shōgai to zōkei* (Special Exhibition: Arts of Buddha Sakyamuni), (Nara: Nara National Museum, 1984), no. 53. For a Chinese prototype believed by some scholars to date to the Southern Song, see *Higashi "Ajia" no Hotoke-tachi* (Buddhist Images of East Asia), (Nara: Nara National Museum, 1996), no. 151. In later Japanese Nirvana paintings, more than one type of "bull," "ox," or water buffalo is sometimes depicted; in a version by Reisai (fl. 1430–1450) in Daizōkyōji temple, three different "bulls" are shown, one of which is green in color like the bull in the *Jin'ōji engi emaki* (see note 18 above). See Tanaka Ichimatsu, *Kaō, Mokuan, Minchō* (The Ink Painters Kaō, Mokuan, and Minchō), Suiboku bijutsu taikei, 5 (Tokyo: Kōdansha, 1974), no. 113. For other examples of Nirvana paintings, see Nakano Genzō, *Nehan-zu* (Depictions of the Parinirvana of the Buddha), Nihon no bijutsu, 268 (September 1988).

Designed to be viewed from right to left in typical
Japanese fashion, the scroll begins at the back of the volume.

Postscript

Even if a mountain obstructs one's view, seeing smoke, one knows there is a fire.
Even if a fence obstructs one's view, seeing the horns, one knows there is an ox.
 Just so, those ancient sages, never taking a step, immobile—
 Oh, where have they gone?
 I have copied the text three times, to avoid any mistakes.

 It is lowing and lowing.
 Its hooves and horns are clearly visible, and one can get hold of it.
 Do not try to distinguish it from its shadow and hoofprints.
 Ten oxen are fundamentally the same as one stand of firs.

 In the Year of the Fifth Tiger of the Kōan Era [1278],
  On the sixteenth day of the eighth month
   I am inscribing the postscript of the Ten Pictures of the Ox.
   [signed]—(?)-gi

嗚呼也又嗚呼也　蹄角分明觸霧道

吳官按身分影跡　十牛元是一毛同

弘安代寅仲秋之後一日書干

十牛圖後　義口

隔山見煙便知是火

隔墻見角便知是牛

古人如是不動一步

當下休去何也吽。

一字三寫烏馬成馬

POEM

He enters the city barefoot, with chest exposed.
Covered in dust and ashes, smiling broadly.
No need for the magic powers of the gods and immortals,
Just let the dead tree bloom again.

10. Entering the City with Hands Hanging Down

COMMENTARY

The brushwood gate of the hut is closed,
    Even thousands of sages could not know what is within.

I conceal the beauty of where I am,
    And refuse to follow the path
    Of the wise men of the past.

Holding my wine gourd, I enter the market;
    Using my stick I return home.

Wine shop and fish market
    Become Buddha
    And enlighten me.

直教枯木放花開

第十入鄽垂手序

柴門獨掩千聖不知

埋自己之風光貧前

賢之途轍提瓢入市

策杖還家酒肆魚行

化令成佛

頌曰

露胸跣足入鄽來

抹土塗灰笑滿腮

不用神仙真秘訣

POEM

In returning to the fundamentals and going back to the source,
    I had to work so hard.

Perhaps it would be better to be blind and deaf.

Being in the hut, I do not see what is outside.

The river flowing tranquilly,
    The flower simply being red.

9. Return to the Fundamentals, Back to the Source

COMMENTARY

Pure and clear from the beginning, free of any dust.

From the realm of non-being,
    One observes the rising and falling [transitory changes]
      In the world of forms.

It is not the same as magic, so why need one embellish?

The water is blue, the mountain green.
    Calmly seated, one observes the ups and downs of the world.

水
自
茫
茫
花
自
紅

第九返本還源序

本来清淨不愛一塵

觀有相之榮枯塵無

為之殼窠不同幻化

豈假修持水綠山青

坐觀成敗

頌曰

返本還源已貴功

爭如直下若盲聾

庵中不見庵前物

POEM

Whip, rope, man, and ox,
     All are non-existent.

The blue sky being vast,
     No message can be heard,

Just as the snowflake cannot last
     In the flaming red furnace.

After this state,
     One can join the ancient teachers.

8. The Ox and the Man, Both Forgotten

COMMENTARY

All confusion fallen away,
    The enlightened mind is not there.

No need to linger in the realm of Buddha;
    But always pass quickly
    Through the realm of no Buddha.

Not lingering in either realm, one cannot be seen.

Hundreds of birds bringing flowers
    Are an embarrassment.
    [Praise is meaningless.]

到_テ此_ニ方_ニ能_ク合_ニ祖宗

第八人牛倶忘序

九情脱落聖意皆空
有佛處不用遨遊無
佛處急須走過兩頭
不着千眼難窺百鳥
衘花一場懊儜

頌曰

鞭索人牛盡屬空
碧天遼闊信難通
紅爐焰上爭容雪

POEM

Riding on the ox, he has come home.
There is no ox there, and he is at ease.
Although the sun is high, he is still dreamy,
The whip and rope abandoned in the thatched hut.

7. The Ox Forgotten, the Man Remains

COMMENTARY

There is only one law, and the ox is hypothetical.

The rabbit snare is not the rabbit, nor the fishnet the fish.
[Once the rabbit or fish is caught, the trap or net is no longer needed.]

Like gold separated from dross,
      Or the moon emerging from a cloud,

The ray of light has been shining
      Since before the beginning of time.

鞭繩空頓畫堂間

第七志牛存人序

法無二法牛且為宗
喩蹄光之異名顯筌
魚之差別如金出鑛
似月離雲一道寒光
威音劫外

頌曰

騎牛已得到家山
牛也空号人也閑
紅日三竿猶作夢

POEM

Riding the bull, I leisurely wander toward home.
Exotic flute melodies echo through sunset clouds,
Each beat and each tune indescribably profound.
No words are needed for those who understand music.

6. Riding the Ox and Returning Home

COMMENTARY

The struggle is over,

    No more gain or loss.

Sing the village woodcutter's song,

    And play on the flute the tunes of children,

Sitting sideways on top of the ox,

    Eyes fixed on the clouds in the sky,

If called, not turning back,

    Or if stopped, not ever staying.

知音何必鼓唇牙

第六騎牛歸家序

干戈巳罷得共還無
唱樵子之村歌吹兒
童之野曲身橫牛上
目視雲霄呼喚不回
撈籠不住

頌曰

騎牛迤邐欲還家
羌笛聲聲送晚霞
一拍一歌無限意

POEM

One does not let go of the whip or the rope,
Afraid it will stray and choose the dusty mist.
A well-tended ox becomes gentle,
And even with no rope will follow people by himself.

5. Herding the Ox

COMMENTARY

As one becomes conscious, more thoughts follow.

Awakening to one's senses, the truth is achieved,
But in losing one's senses, delusion prevails.

Delusion is not caused by the object
But is only created by the subject.
[Delusions originate in us, not in the world around us.]

Pull tightly on the nose-rope
And do not hesitate.

羈鎖無拘自逐人

第五牧牛序

前思繞起後念相随
由覺以成真在迷而
爲妻不由境有唯自
心生鼻索牢牽不容
擬議
頌曰
鞭索時時不離身
恐伏縱步惹埃塵
相将牧得純和也

POEM

With all my energy, I seize the ox.

His will is strong, and his power inexhaustible,
       He cannot be tamed easily.

Sometimes he charges to the high plateau,

And there he stays, deep in the mist.

4. Catching the Ox

COMMENTARY

The ox lived in obscurity in the field for so long,
    But I found him today.

While I am distracted by the beautiful scenery,
    And the difficult chase,
        The ox is longing for fragrant grass.

His mind is still stubborn,
    And his wild nature yet remains.

If I wish him tamed, I must whip him.

又入煙雲深處居

第四得牛序

久埋郊外今日逢渠

由境勝以難追戀芳

藂而不已頑心尚勇

野性猶存欲得純和

必加鞭楚

頌曰

竭盡神通獲得渠

心強力壯卒難除

有時纔到高原上

POEM

A bush warbler sings upon a branch,
Warm sun, soft breezes, green willows on the bank.
Nowhere can the ox escape to hide,
But those majestic horns are difficult to draw.

3. Seeing the Ox

COMMENTARY

Led by the sound, one starts out on the path
      And at first sight of it, one sees the origin of things.

All of one's senses work harmoniously,
      Their presence manifest in all the things one usually does.

Just like the taste of salt in water, or the glue in dye,
[It is definitely there, but is not discreet.]

If one's eyes are wide open,
      One sees it [truth] clearly, not as something else.

第三見牛序

從聲得入、見處逢源
六根門着、着無差動
用中頭頭顯露水中
鹽味色裏膠青眼上
眉毛非是它物

頌曰
黃鸝枝上一聲聲
日暖風咊岸柳青
只此更無迴避處

POEM

By the water, and under the trees,
        There are numerous traces.

Fragrant grasses grow thickly,
        Did you see the ox?

Even in the depths of the distant mountain forest,

How could the upturned nostrils of the ox be concealed?

2. Seeing the Footprints of the Ox

COMMENTARY

Relying on sutras, one comprehends the meaning,
　　And studying the doctrines, one finds some traces.

As it becomes clear that differently shaped metal vessels
　　Are all made from the same piece of metal,
　　　　One realizes that the myriad entities [one thinks one sees]
　　　　Are formulated by oneself.

Unless one can separate the orthodox from the heretics,
　　How can one distinguish the true from the untrue?

Not having entered the gate as yet,
　　At least one has noticed the traces.

遼天鼻孔怎蔵侘

第二見跡序

依經解義、閲教知蹤。明衆器為一金、體萬物為自己。正邪不辨、真偽美別。末入此門、權為見跡。

頌曰

水邊林下跡偏多
芳草離披見也麼
縱是深山更深處

POEM

One aimlessly pushes the grasses aside in search.
The rivers are wide, the mountains far away,
          And the path becomes longer.

Exhausted and dispirited,

One hears only the late autumn cicadas
          Shrilling in the maple woods.

1. Searching for the Ox

COMMENTARY

Nothing has been lost in the first place,
    So what is the use of searching?

By refusing to come to one's senses,
    One becomes separated from
        And eventually loses sight of what one seeks.

Home grows more and more distant,
    And one comes to many crossroads.

Thoughts of gain and loss burn like fire,
    And ideas of right and wrong
        Rise up like the blade of a sword.

岐路俄差得共機非
是非鋒起

頌曰

茫茫撥草去追尋
水闊山遙路更深
力盡神疲無覓處
但聞楓樹晩蟬吟

The *Ten Oxherding Songs*

第一尋牛序

從来不失何用追尋

曲背覺以成疎在向

處而遂去家山漸遠

and the oxherder finally become invisible, signifying the disappearance of both mind and doctrine. The principle is quite correct, but the teaching method still retains the metaphor of travel [progression]. As a result, it puzzles those with limited abilities, and confuses those who are mediocre. Some fear losing their sense of the [physical] world, while others scream and fall back upon their preconceived ideas.

From my point of view, the ten poems by Chan master Zigong [Guoan] were based on the works of his predecessors [like Qingjiu], but they were created from Zigong's own heart, each poem sparkling like a jewel, and all reflecting one another. From the beginning when one is lost, to the end when one has returned to the ultimate source, all [of the poems] correspond very well to the different needs of people, like giving food to the hungry and water to the thirsty.

Therefore I, Ciyuan, will look for the essence and write a summary of each poem, just like a jellyfish searching for food by relying upon the eyes of a shrimp.

Beginning with the search for the ox and ending with the entry into the city may make unnecessary waves and cause the horns of the ox to protrude. If there is no mind to seek, where is the need to search for the ox? And to conclude the search by entering the city—is this the work of evil spirits? Perhaps not having obtained the approval of the ancestors will bring misfortune to coming generations, but while trying not to be absurd, I am going to comment on the [following] verses.

Preface, by the Monk Ciyuan

[On] the Ten Oxherding Pictures
by the Monk Guoan of Mt. Liang, Dingzhou

In any case, all buddhas are the ultimate origin of things, and all sentient beings have Buddhahood within themselves. When one is deluded, one can sink into the three realms of illusion, but one can also be awakened and avoid being reborn into one of the four forms of life. Thus, there are those who could be enlightened and become buddhas, and those who are deluded.

For this very reason, the ancient sage [Buddha Shakyamuni] was compassionate enough to prepare a variety of paths [to enlightenment]. There is the principle of the whole and its parts, enlightenment can be sudden or gradual, and the explanation can be from general to meticulous and from shallow to deep.

At the end of his life, when Shaka [Shakyamuni] blinked his green lotuslike eyes, his first disciple [Mahakasyapa] smiled and nodded. This was how the words for the true teaching were spread. Whether heavenly beings or human beings, in this world or in any other realm, those who attain [understanding of] the principle will transcend lineage or status, just as the flight path of a bird leaves no footprints. But one who is concerned only with facts becomes stagnant with phrases and at a loss for words, as if the divine tortoise had gotten stuck in the mud.

Recently, Chan [Zen] Master Qingjiu, observing the potentials of people, created the parable of oxherding in order to treat their maladies; he drew it and taught it according to varying circumstances. It begins with the color of the ox gradually changing from black to white, indicating the change from non-achievement of one's full potential to the final fulfillment of that potential—which is shown to be the ultimate source [enlightenment]. Both the ox

如救飢渇慈遠　是以探尋妙義採拾
玄後如水母以壽食伏海蝦而為目
初自尋牛終至入鄽奮起波瀾横生
頭角尚無心而可覓何有牛而可尋
洎至入鄽是何魔魅況是祖祢不了
欻及兒孫不揆荒塘試為提唱

迷言若靈龜而拽尾間有清居禪師
觀衆生之根器應病施方作牧牛以
爲圖隨機設教初從漸白顯力量之
末先次至純真表根機之漸熟乃到
人牛不見故標心法雙亡其理也已
盡根源其法也尚存巢笠遂使淺根
凝悞中下杉絵或疑之洛空亡或愛
作墮常見今觀則公禪師擬前賢之
復範出自己之胷襟十頌佳篇交光
相映初從共慶終至還源善應羣機

住鼎州梁山廓庵和尚十牛圖

夫諸佛真源衆生本有因迷也流淪
三界由悟也頓出四生所以有諸佛
而可成有衆生而可作是故先賢悲
悲憫廣設多途理出偏圓教興頓漸
従麁及細自浅至深末後目瞬青蓮
引得頭陀微笑正法眼藏自此流通
天上人間此方佗界得其理也超宗
越格如鳥道而無蹤得其事也滞句

a Zen monk. His signature, "[Ko?]gi" appears at the close of the postscript, which also contains the date of the completion of the piece. The date, which corresponds to 1278, is recorded as the Year of the Fifth Tiger (one of the twelve signs of the Chinese zodiac), in the Kōan Era (1278–88). Era names like "Kōan" were determined by the imperial court and did not represent reigns of individual emperors until the Meiji period (1868–1912). The lunar calendar used in ancient and medieval Japan differed slightly from the Western calendar in its arrangement of the twelve months of the year, the "first month" being roughly one month ahead of our January. (The Japanese adopted the Gregorian calendar in 1873.)

—SW

A Note on the Burke Handscroll

The handscroll of the *Ten Oxherding Songs* was created in ink and mineral pigments on paper, and measures 1 ft. ¼ in. (31 cm) in height by 20 ft. 6 in. (624.6 cm) in length. Each of the sheets of paper pasted together to form the scroll measures approximately 9⅞ in. (25 cm) in length, which suggests that work was made originally in book form, with the pages folded in an accordion fashion. A frontispiece of silk, with a woven silk tie, protects the handscroll when it is rolled up for storage.

Like virtually all Japanese books and handscrolls from ancient to modern times, the *Ten Oxherding Songs* is meant to be viewed from right to left. The written sections, inscribed in vertical columns, are read from the top to bottom of each column, moving from right to left. All of the text—preface, poems, commentaries, and postscript—was written in Chinese, in standard (noncursive) script. Some of the Chinese characters are accompanied by tiny, angular *furigana*: letters of the Japanese phonetic syllabary (*katakana*) written to the right of the corresponding ideographs to indicate their correct pronunciation.

The artist of the painted scenes is unknown; the calligrapher, who inscribed the preface, commentary and poems, and postscript, was probably

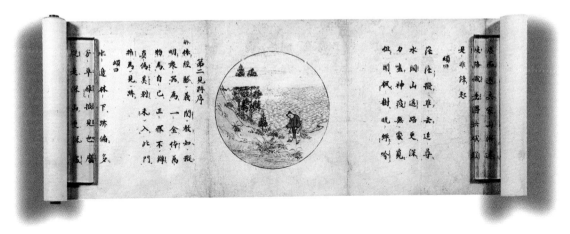

The Scroll